EXPLORING AFRICA

Continents of the World
Geography Series

By
MICHAEL KRAMME, Ph.D.

COPYRIGHT © 2002 Mark Twain Media, Inc.

ISBN 1-58037-210-4

Printing No. CD-1556

Mark Twain Media, Inc., Publishers
Distributed by Carson-Dellosa Publishing Company, Inc.

Map Source: Mountain High Maps® Copyright © 1993 Digital Wisdom, Inc.

Table of Contents

The Continents

A continent is a large land-mass completely or mostly surrounded by water. Geographers list seven continents: North America, South America, Europe, Asia, Africa, Australia, and Antarctica. Greenland and the India-Pakistan area are sometimes referred to as "subcontinents." Madagascar and the Seychelles Islands are often called "microcontinents." The island groups in the Pacific Ocean are called "Oceania," but they are not considered a continent.

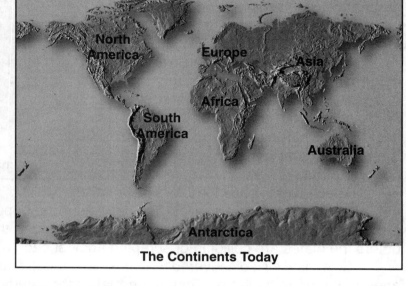

The Continents Today

The continents make up just over 29 percent of the earth's surface. They occupy about 57,100,000 square miles (148,000,000 sq. km). More than 65 percent of the land area is in the Northern Hemisphere.

HOW WERE THE CONTINENTS FORMED?

For many years, Europeans believed the continents were formed by a catastrophe or series of catastrophes, such as floods, earthquakes, and volcanoes. In 1596, a Dutch mapmaker, Abraham Ortelius, noted that the Americas' eastern coasts and the western coasts of Europe and Africa looked as if they fit together. He proposed that once they had been joined but later were torn apart.

Many years later, a German named Alfred Lothar Wegener published a book in which he explained his theory of the "**Continental Drift**." Wegener, like Ortelius, believed that the earth originally had one super continent. He named it **Pangaea** from the Greek word meaning "all lands." He believed that the large landmass was a lighter rock that floated on a heavier rock, like ice floats on water.

Wegener's theory stated that the landmasses were still moving at a rate of about one yard each century. Wegener believed that Pangaea existed in the Permian Age. Then Pangaea slowly divided into two continents, the upper part, **Laurasia**, and the lower, **Gondwanaland**, during the Triassic Age.

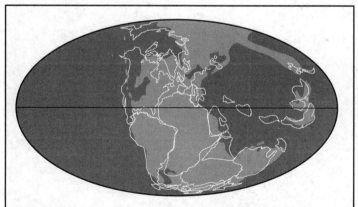

Wegener's theoretical continent, Pangaea, during the Permian Age (white outlines indicate current continents)

By the Jurassic Age, the land-masses had moved into what we could recognize as the seven continents, although they were still located near each other. Eventually, the continents "drifted" to their present locations.

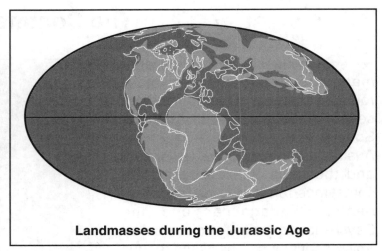

Landmasses during the Jurassic Age

Most scientists had been in agreement on the continental drift theory until researchers in the 1960s discovered several major mountain ranges on the ocean floor. These mountains suggested that the earth's crust consists of about 20 slabs or **plates**.

These discoveries lead to a new theory, "**Plate Tectonics**," which has become more popular. This theory suggests that these plates move a few inches each year. In some places the plates are moving apart, while in others the plates are colliding or scraping against each other.

Scientists also discovered that most volcanoes and earthquakes occur along the boundaries of the various plates. They hope that further study will help them increase their understanding of Earth's story.

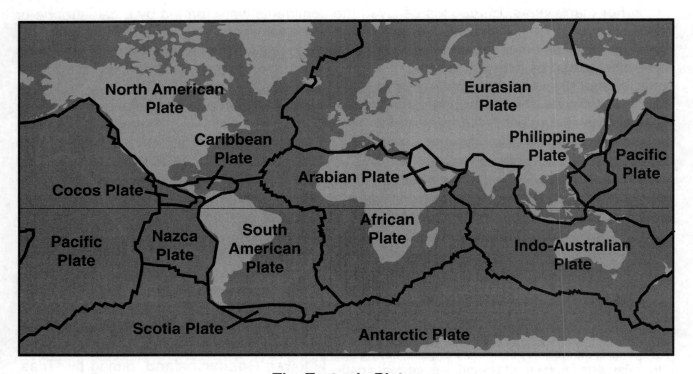

The Tectonic Plates

Name: _____ Date: _____

Questions for Consideration

1. What is a continent? _____

   _____

2. The continents make up what percentage of the earth's surface?

   _____

3. What was the name of Wegener's theory?

   _____

4. What is the name of the newer theory that replaced Wegener's?

   _____

5. What two natural happenings occur near the boundaries of the plates?

   _____

Map Project

On the map below, label all seven of the continents.

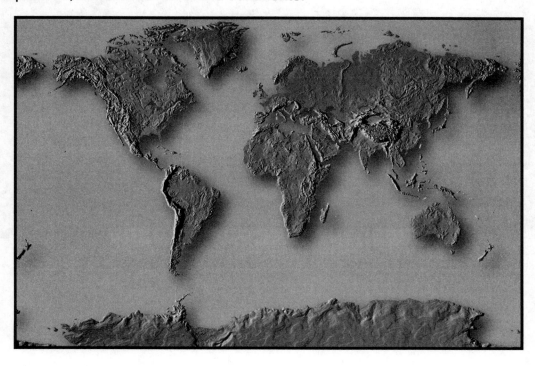

Name: _____ Date: _____

Outline Map of Africa

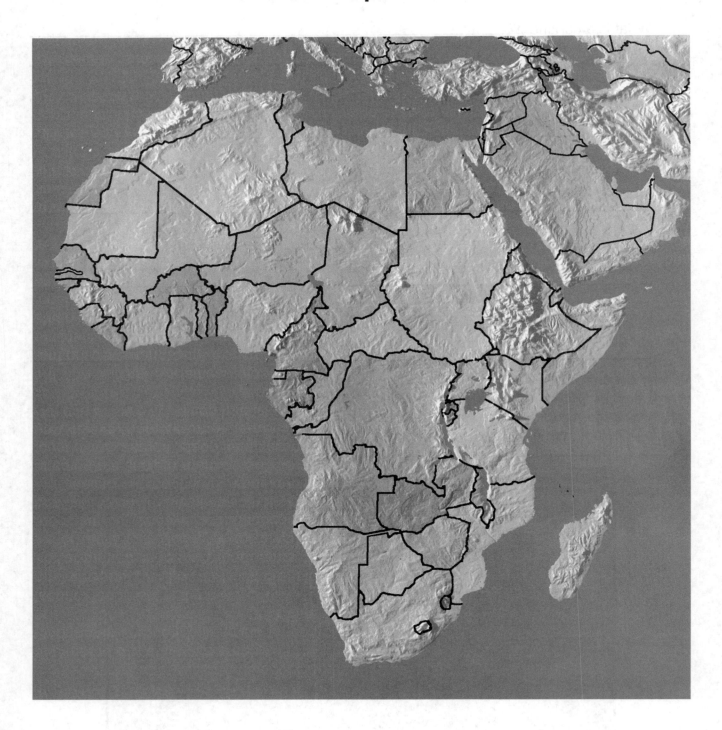

The Continent of Africa

Africa is the second-largest continent; only Asia is larger. Africa covers over 11,677,000 square miles (30,243,000 sq. km). It contains 23 percent of the world's total land area and is three times as large as the United States.

The equator divides Africa in half. Africa's northernmost point is 35° North, and its southernmost point is 36° South.

Africa is almost completely surrounded by water. The northern coast is on the Mediterranean Sea. The western coast is on the Atlantic Ocean, and the eastern coast is bordered by the Red Sea, the Arabian Sea, and the Indian Ocean. A small land border joins Egypt and Israel.

Africa includes several islands. The largest island is Madagascar, located off the southeast coast.

The continent is mainly plateau land. It does have narrow coastal plains and a few mountain ranges.

The Sahara is the world's largest desert. It covers over 3,500,000 square miles (9,065,000 sq. km). The Sahara covers one-fourth of the continent. It cuts through the northern part of Africa, dividing the continent into northern and southern regions. The northern regions are much more highly developed.

Southern Africa also has desert terrain. The Namib Desert and the Kalahari Desert are located in Namibia and Botswana.

The major rivers of Africa are the Nile and the Congo (also called the Zaire). The Nile is the world's longest river. It has a length of 4,160 miles (6,695 km). The Congo River, 2,718 miles long (4,374 km), drains much of central Africa. The Niger River, 2,600 miles long (4,184 km), empties into part of the southern Pacific Ocean known as the Gulf of Guinea.

Lake Victoria is Africa's largest lake. It is the third-largest lake in the world. Lake Victoria covers over 26,800 square miles (69,400 sq. km). One branch of the Nile River begins at Lake Victoria.

The highest point in Africa is Mount Kilimanjaro. It is 19,341 feet (5,895 m) above sea level. The lowest point is Lake Assal, which is 502 feet (153 m) below sea level. Africa contains one of the world's most spectacular waterfalls. They were named the Victoria Falls by the Scottish explorer David Livingstone in honor of Queen Victoria of England. Victoria Falls are on the Zambezi River in Zimbabwe near the border with Zambia.

Name: _____ Date: _____

Questions for Consideration

1. What is the only continent larger than Africa?

   _____

2. What is the world's longest river?

   _____

3. What is the world's largest desert?

   _____

4. What divides Africa almost in half?

   _____

5. For whom were the Victoria Falls named?

   _____

Map Project

Using an atlas or globe and the outline map of Africa (located on page 4), label the following:

Bodies of Water:

The Arabian Sea
The Atlantic Ocean
The Congo (Zaire) River
The Indian Ocean
The Mediterranean Sea
The Nile River
The Red Sea
Lake Victoria

Land Features:

The Cape of Good Hope
The equator
The Kalahari Desert
Madagascar
Mount Kilimanjaro
The Sahara Desert
Victoria Falls

DID YOU KNOW?

The Sahara is the world's largest and hottest desert. It stretches 3,000 miles (4,828 km) from the Atlantic Ocean to the Red Sea. It is larger than the entire continent of Australia.

Africa's Climate

Africa has a variety of climate conditions. Each of these various climates remains stable. Much of Africa is in a tropical zone, and a tropical zone's climate tends to remains stable. The continent has few mountain ranges acting as barriers, and several ocean currents help maintain uniform climate features.

Average African temperatures range from 94°F (34°C) in Ethiopia to 51°F (11°C) in Morocco. The average precipitation ranges from 404 inches (10,261 mm) in Cameroon to 0.1 inches (2.5 mm) in the Sudan.

With some exceptions, in regions to the north of the equator, the rainy season is from April to September. South of the equator, the rainy season is from October to March. Regions near the equator have year-round rain.

Africa's mildest climate conditions

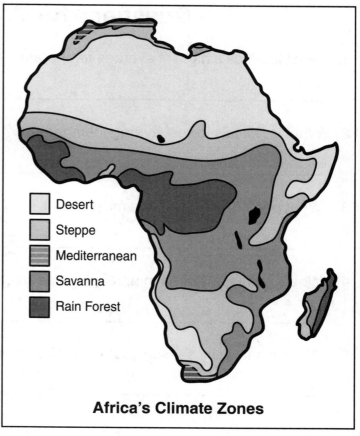

Desert
Steppe
Mediterranean
Savanna
Rain Forest

Africa's Climate Zones

are in the northwest and southwest regions of the continent. These Mediterranean climate zones have mild temperatures, wet winters, and dry summers.

The central part of the continent and much of the island of Madagascar include tropical rain forests. In the rain forest areas, the average temperature is 80°F (27°C). The average rainfall each year is 70 inches (1,778 mm).

North and south of the rainfall area is a tropical savanna climate. A **savanna** is a hot region like a tropical forest; however, it only receives major rainfall for about half the year and has a dry season the other half.

Farther away from the equator, both to the north and the south, the regions have a drier climate known as a **steppe** climate zone. The rainfall in the steppe zone is about 15 inches (381 mm) per year. Most of the rain in the steppe arrives in one season.

Africa also has massive desert regions. In the Sahara, Horn, Kalahari, and Namib Deserts, the rainfall is less than 10 inches (254 mm) each year. The desert temperatures range from over 90°F (32°C) in the summer season to below freezing in the winter season.

DID YOU KNOW?

The hottest temperature (in the shade) ever recorded was 136.4°F (58°C) in Libya in 1922.

Name: _____ Date: _____

Questions for Consideration

1. What is Africa's highest average temperature?

   _____

2. What is Africa's lowest average temperature?

   _____

3. What part of Africa gets the most rainfall?

   _____

4. When is the rainy season north of the equator?

   _____

5. When is the rainy season south of the equator?

   _____

Climate Zones

Describe the following climate zones. Use a dictionary, if necessary.

1. Desert _____

   _____

2. Mediterranean _____

   _____

3. Savanna _____

   _____

4. Steppe _____

   _____

5. Tropical rain forest _____

   _____

Africa's Resources

Africa is perhaps the richest continent in natural resources. It contains many of the world's largest mineral reserves.

Africa has the largest reserves of titanium, uranium, and radium in the world. It also has about one-half of the world's gold, and well over one-half of the world's supply of diamonds.

It also provides about 25 percent of the world's chromite (used for the hardening of steel).

Africa contains about 20 percent of the world's copper and 50 percent of the world's cobalt deposits.

Other major mineral resources include bauxite (the ore from which aluminum is extracted), iron ore, lead, magnesium, nickel, phosphates (used for fertilizer), platinum, tin, and zinc.

The continent also contains major deposits of clays, mica, sulfur, salt, graphite, limestone, and gypsum. The limestone and gypsum reserves help supply a major concrete manufacturing industry.

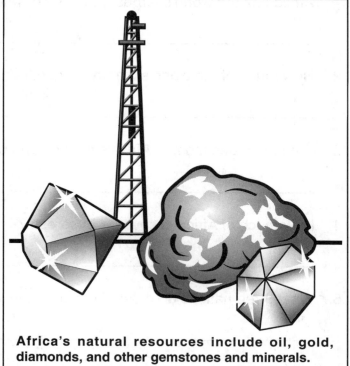

Africa's natural resources include oil, gold, diamonds, and other gemstones and minerals.

Africa also has many large reserves of fossil fuels. The continent contains some deposits of coal and natural gas, as well as major deposits of petroleum. Libya, Nigeria, Algeria, and the western coast are the major locations of Africa's petroleum industries.

Most of Africa's exports are minerals. South Africa contributes about one-half of the continent's mineral income. Gold and diamond mining are the largest industries there.

Most of Africa's mineral and petroleum operations are managed by foreign nations. However, the African governments are working to increase native ownership.

One-fifth of Africa is covered with forests. However, very little of the forests are of commercial value. A few rare hardwoods, such as mahogany, are exported. In the past, much of the forests has been burned as fuel. The forestry industry has grown in recent years. Unfortunately, as the forestry industry grows, deforestation is becoming a serious problem in several regions.

Freshwater fishing and ocean fishing are done for local consumption. The number of fish farms is increasing. Commercial fishing off Africa's coast is done by Japan, Russia, and the United States.

Name: _____ Date: _____

Questions for Consideration

1. Africa has the world's largest reserves of what three minerals?

   _____

2. How much of the world's diamonds does Africa supply?

   _____

3. Who manages most of Africa's mineral and petroleum industries?

   _____

4. How much of Africa is covered by forests?

   _____

5. What three nations do most of the commercial fishing off Africa's coast?

   _____

Matching

Match the item in the left column with the most closely related term in the right column:

_____ 1. Bauxite   a. Aluminum

_____ 2. Chromite   b. Cement

_____ 3. Gypsum   c. Fertilizer

_____ 4. Mahogany   d. Hardening steel

_____ 5. Phosphates   e. Hardwood

DID YOU KNOW?

Cacao trees grow in much of Africa. Huge pods are cut from the trees, and then the beans inside the pods are dried to make chocolate and cocoa.

Africa's Industries

Africa's foreign trade consists of about 52 percent exports and 48 percent imports. Most of the trade is with European nations, especially Britain and France.

Agriculture is Africa's largest industry. Most of the production goes to feeding the continent's population. However, the population is growing faster than the agricultural output.

African farmers grow some crops for export. Major export crops include bananas, cacao, coffee, tea, and tobacco. In recent years, land has been cleared for plantation crops, such as rubber and palms (for oil).

In northern Africa, barley, citrus fruits, corn, dates, oats, olives, wheat, and a variety of vegetables are the major crops. Herds of goats and sheep are also raised in the region.

In the savanna regions, crops include corn (maize), cotton, beans,

Most of Africa's crops are used to feed its growing population.

cassava, sweet potatoes, millet, peanuts, sorghum, and soybeans. Herds of camels, cattle, pigs, poultry, and sheep live in the region.

South of the savanna, outside the rain forest areas, rice, yams, cassava, okra, and bananas are raised.

Mining and petroleum are both growing industries. Africa supplies much of the world's gold, diamonds, copper, and other valuable minerals. Industries for the extracting and processing of minerals and petroleum are mainly located in South Africa.

Africa was the location of very little manufacturing for many years. Its raw materials were exported to Europe, and finished goods were then imported at high prices. This kept much of the continent in poverty. Since their independence, many of the national governments have encouraged the local manufacturing of items, especially building materials, textiles, vehicle tires, and canned goods. Heavy industries, including the manufacturing of machines and transportation equipment, have also increased, especially in South Africa.

Africa has a tremendous potential for the development of hydroelectric power, which uses moving water to create electricity. This resource has been underdeveloped in the past. Since 1960, major hydroelectric projects, including the Aswan and Cabor Bassa Dams, have been constructed.

Transportation is another industry likely to develop further in the future. Few paved roads exist, nor are there many roads linking the various nations within the continent. New railways and transcontinental highways are planned or currently under construction.

Name: _____ Date: _____

Questions for Consideration

1. Does Africa export or import more?

   _____

2. What is Africa's largest industry?

   _____

3. With what is this industry unable to keep pace?

   _____

4. Where are most of Africa's heavy industries?

   _____

5. For what type of power does Africa have the greatest potential?

   _____

Africa's Exports

The narrative on Africa's industries lists several crops grown for export. For each of the crops listed below, place an "X" before the name if it is a major export crop from Africa and an "O" if it is not.

_____ 1. Apples   _____ 6. Potatoes

_____ 2. Bananas   _____ 7. Soybeans

_____ 3. Cacao   _____ 8. Spinach

_____ 4. Carrots   _____ 9. Tea

_____ 5. Coffee   _____ 10. Tobacco

DID YOU KNOW?
The world's oldest mines are some of the iron ore mines of Swaziland. They are over 4,000 years old.

Africa's Animal Life

Africa is the home to a greater variety of animal life than any other continent.

The savanna is the home to most of the continent's wildlife. Large numbers of antelopes, baboons, cheetahs, elephants, foxes, gazelles, giraffes, hares, hippopotamuses, hyenas, jackals, leopards, lions, monkeys, rhinoceroses, and zebras roam throughout the region.

The northern regions are home to camels, deer, goats, horses, and sheep.

Bats, lemurs, monkeys, flying squirrels, and gorillas live in the rain forest regions.

Most people are familiar with the wild animals of Africa; however, the majority of animals living on the continent are domesticated. Farmers raise large herds of pigs, cattle, goats, and poultry for food.

The numbers of wildlife have decreased considerably in the last several years. Hunting and **poaching** (the illegal killing of animals to sell skins or tusks) have lowered the animal population. Increased farming has decreased the numbers of wildlife in their natural habitats. As more land is used for farming, less is available as a habitat for animals.

Recently, several national parks have been established to help protect species from extinction. The national parks have also encouraged tourists to visit to observe animals in their native habitats. In addition, the development of the national preserves has aided scientists in their study of animal behavior.

Africa is also the home to many destructive insects. Colonies of ants build huge anthills. Termites and locusts plague many areas. Certain mosquitoes carry diseases, including malaria. The tsetse fly transmits sleeping sickness, which affects both humans and animals.

Africa is home to a variety of colorful tropical birds. Pelicans, herons, flamingos, egrets, and storks gather in large numbers. The ostrich is common in the eastern and southern regions. The ibis is native to the Nile Valley and was once worshipped by the ancient Egyptians. Some of the birds are hunted as food. Many of the species of birds are destructive to crops.

Rodents are numerous in Africa. They carry diseases such as cholera and also destroy crops.

African reptiles include lizards, crocodiles, tortoises, and several varieties of snakes. Pythons live in the western region, while boa constrictors inhabit Madagascar. Many of the African snakes are poisonous.

The continent is also host to more than 2,000 species of freshwater fish.

Name: _____ Date: _____

Questions for Consideration

1. What region is home to most of Africa's wildlife?

   _____

2. What is poaching?

   _____

3. What has been established to protect endangered species?

   _____

4. What insect transmits sleeping sickness?

   _____

5. What bird did the ancient Egyptians worship?

   _____

> **DID YOU KNOW?**
>
> Rhinoceros horn is thought by many to have medicinal value. For years, many of the animal were slaughtered for their horns.

For Further Research

Choose one of the animals mentioned in the narrative with which you are less familiar. Write a paragraph in the space below describing this animal. Use at least two sources to help you.

_____

_____

_____

_____

_____

_____

_____

_____

The People of Africa

Africa's population in 2000 was estimated at more than 797 million people. It is the second-largest continent containing one-fifth of the world's land, and yet it has only 12 percent of the world's population. Due in part to advances in medical treatment, the population is increasing at about 2.5 percent each year. It is the world's fastest-growing continent.

Most of Africa's population live in rural areas. Africa has only a dozen cities with populations of over one million. Cairo, Egypt, is Africa's largest city with a population of about six and one-half million people.

Africa is home to a diverse population. There are over 3,000 different ethnic groups in Africa. They speak about 1,000 different languages.

North of the Sahara Desert most of the people are lighter-skinned and are a mixture of Arab and indigenous (originally from a region) people, especially the Berbers. The culture of the northern region is more similar to the Middle East than to the rest of Africa. The region south of the Sahara contains about 70 percent of the total population. These people are darker-skinned and include a variety of ethnic groups, including the Khosian and Pygmies.

Descendants of Europeans are also scattered throughout the continent, since Europeans colonized many of the African countries from the 1500s to the 1900s.

Many of the ethnic groups are linked by kinship. They are often formed into clans. Many outsiders refer to these as "tribes." However, the word *tribe* is not really accurate. Anthropologists (scientists who study human beings, their works, and cultures) prefer to use the term **societies**.

Anthropologists divide African society into six major types based on the primary activity of the members. Some societies include hunters, gatherers, herders (mainly of cattle), fishers, and planters. In modern times, the societies have become much more mixed.

The people of Africa have three major religions. Most Africans believe in Christianity, which has over 327 million followers. The Islamic faith has over 278 million followers, and native traditional religions have over 71 million followers. Most of the traditional religions believe in one major power or spirit and many lesser spirits.

Africa has the lowest literacy rate of any of the continents. Less than half of its people can read and write. The national governments are working hard to improve the nations' standards of education.

Health is another issue of major concern in Africa. It has the highest death rate of any continent. Poor health care, poor diets, and lack of sanitation contribute to the high death rate. AIDS is one of the leading causes of death in many African nations. The African nations and the United Nations are working together to improve living conditions and lessen the effects of diseases.

Name: _____ Date: _____

Questions for Consideration

1. What percentage of the world's population lives in Africa?

   _____

2. What is Africa's largest city?

   _____

3. How many different ethnic groups live in Africa?

   _____

4. What percentage of Africa's population lives south of the Sahara Desert?

   _____

5. What are the three major religious groups in Africa?

   _____

> **DID YOU KNOW?**
>
> English is the official language of Nigeria, but it has over 240 other languages.

Vocabulary

This narrative may contain some words that are less familiar to you. In the space following each word, write its meaning.

1. Diverse _____

   _____

2. Indigenous _____

   _____

3. Kinship _____

   _____

4. Anthropologist _____

   _____

5. Literacy _____

   _____

African Culture

Africa has a very diverse culture. Much of its culture relates to ethnic groups. All of the arts in the northern regions have strong Islamic influences. The arts south of the Sahara Desert have a more traditional, native influence.

Many of the artists specialize in making items for other members of their society. Major types of art include: masks, pottery, textiles, beadwork, and sculpture.

Much of the art serves a useful purpose, in addition to being pleasing in appearance. Baskets, pottery, eating utensils, and textiles are examples of this. Other African art, especially masks and headdresses, is also used in religious ceremonies and other rituals.

African artists use a variety of materials, including gold, brass, leather, ivory, beads, and feathers, to create jewelry and sculptures.

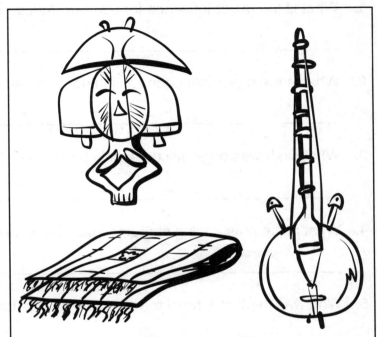

African artists and craftspeople make items for practical and ceremonial use, such as masks, cloth, and musical instruments.

African textiles have both woven and printed designs. Many of the designs indicate the status of the wearer. The Kente cloth was a special design once reserved for royalty. It was a brightly-colored cloth with gold threads woven into its design.

Traditional music and dance are important parts of African daily life as well as celebrations and religious ceremonies. Often songs accompany work tasks.

Rhythm is the most outstanding characteristic of African music. Often the rhythm of a selection is emphasized by hand-clapping. Drums and other percussion instruments are an important part of African music. However, a wide range of horns and stringed instruments are also often used.

Much of African music includes group performance. Call and response is often used in African music. The leader sings a phrase and the chorus then sings a phrase in response.

African literature came from a long oral tradition. Stories were told by members of one generation to the next. Eventually, these stories were written down. One of the most famous stories was the epic of *Sundiata,* which comes from the thirteenth century.

Many African poets, novelists, and authors of nonfiction have been widely published and read in recent years. Three African writers have received Nobel prizes for literature: Wole Soyina (1986), Naguib Mahfouz (1988), and Nadine Gordimer (1991).

Many of Africa's artists are returning to native themes, while others are combining older and modern styles. African art and music are currently receiving greater worldwide attention and appreciation.

Name: _____ Date: _____

Questions for Consideration

1. What is the major influence for northern African art?

   _____

2. What is the major influence for southern African art?

   _____

3. What cloth was originally used only by royalty?

   _____

4. What is the outstanding characteristic of African music?

   _____

5. Who was the first African to win a Nobel Prize for literature?

   _____

Matching

Match the item in the left column with the most closely related term in the right column.

_____ 1. An epic story   a. Hand-clapping

_____ 2. Type of cloth   b. Headdresses

_____ 3. Nobel Prize   c. Kente

_____ 4. Rhythm   d. Sundiata

_____ 5. Ritual   e. Soyina

DID YOU KNOW?

The pyramids of Egypt were built as tombs over 4,000 years ago. They are still Africa's largest buildings.

The Nations of Northern Africa

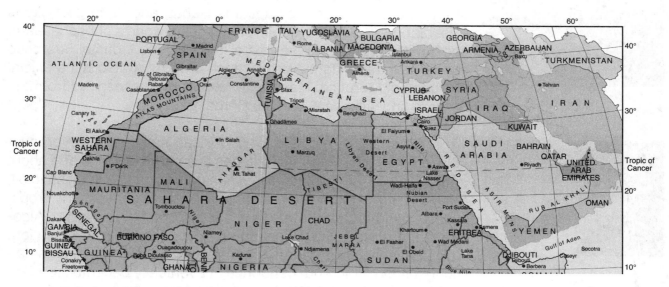

Northern Africa is bounded on the north by the Mediterranean Sea, on the west by the Atlantic Ocean, on the east by the Red Sea, and on the south by the Sahara Desert. The region includes the countries of Morocco, Algeria, Libya, and Egypt.

This region is Africa's most densely populated. The prominent ethnic groups include the Arabs and the Berbers. The Berbers probably immigrated into the region from Asia over 4,000 years ago. The Berbers and Arabs formed an alliance that became the Moorish Empire about A.D. 700. Because of the Arab and Islamic influences, this region of Africa is more like the Middle Eastern region than the area of Africa south of the Sahara. Africa's northern coast has a warm Mediterranean climate that is popular with tourists.

Egypt is northern Africa's most populated country. Its capital city, Cairo, has over 13,000,000 people, making it Africa's largest city. The Nile River has been important to the lives of the Egyptians for over 6,000 years. The ancient Egyptian civilization grew along the banks of the Nile. Many of the ancient structures, especially the pyramids, tombs, and temples, bring thousands of tourists to the country each year. Today, half of Egypt's population lives in Cairo and Alexandria, while the other half lives in small towns and villages along the banks of the river. Egypt's major products include cotton, textiles, chemicals, and petroleum products.

Libya is mainly desert. Most of the population lives on a narrow strip of land bordering the Mediterranean Sea. Libya's capital and largest city is Tripoli. It was ruled by the Turks for approximately 500 years. It became an Italian colony in 1912 and then was ruled by Britain and France after World War I until it gained its independence in 1951. Libya has huge oil reserves, and petroleum is its major product. Libya has been under the military rule of Muammar el-Quaddafi since 1969. Quaddafi's radical political views include the use of terrorism. Relations between Libya and much of the Western world, including the United States, have been hostile.

Morocco has a long coast on the Atlantic Ocean and a short one on the Mediterranean Sea. The Atlas Mountains cover the center of the country. Morocco's capital is Rabat, and its largest city is Casablanca. Morocco produces most of the world's phosphate and phosphate fertilizer. It also has a large fishing industry. Morocco gained its independence from France in 1956. Arabic is the official language of Morocco. Many of its people are descended from the Berbers and still speak various Berber dialects.

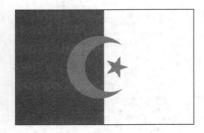

Algeria is one of the larger African nations; however, over 90 percent of it is desert. Algeria has two major oil fields and about 95 percent of all its exports are oil and natural gas. In addition to oil, Algeria is also a major exporter of wine. Algeria grows many crops, such as barley, wheat, citrus fruits, dates, and figs. However, Algerian farmers cannot grow enough food to support the population, so the nation imports a large amount of food. Although Algeria had a long, bitter war for independence, it eventually became independent from France in 1962. France and Algeria have maintained a strong trading connection since independence.

Tunisia is the smallest nation in northern Africa. It covers 63,170 square miles (163,610 sq. km). Tunisia was the location of the ancient city of Carthage. It became independent from France in 1956. Tunisia's capital is Tunis. Tunisia's major exports include iron ore, lead, oil, phosphates, and zinc. Tunisian farmers grow grains, grapes, sugar beets, and olives. In recent years, tourism has become a major industry.

DID YOU KNOW?

The Islamic University in Fez, Morocco, is the world's oldest university. It was founded in A.D. 859.

Name: _____ Date: _____

Questions for Consideration

1. What is Africa's northern boundary?

   _____

2. What are northern Africa's two major ethnic groups?

   _____

3. What river was important for the development of civilization in Egypt?

   _____

4. What is the capital of Libya?

   _____

5. What country produces most of the world's phosphate?

   _____

Map Project

On the map below, label the following:

Algeria	Egypt	Mediterranean Sea	Red Sea
Atlantic Ocean	Libya	Morocco	Tunisia

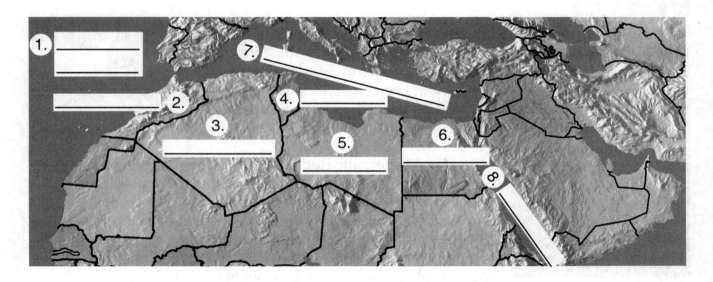

The Nations of West and Central Africa

The nations of west and central Africa include: Benin, Burkina Faso, Chad, Cameroon, Central African Republic, Congo (formerly Zaire), Gabon, Gambia, Ghana, Guinea, Guinea-Bissau, Ivory Coast, Liberia, Mauritania, Mali, Niger, Nigeria, Rwanda, Senegal, Sierra Leone, and Togo. Many of the nations of the region were European colonies until after the 1950s when they gained their independence.

The region has also been the site of many political uprisings and rapid changes of governments. A large portion of this region is covered by desert. A good share of the region is part of the Congo Basin, which is drained by the Congo (Zaire) River. Most of the population of the region live along the Atlantic Ocean coast.

Cameroon was once the site of slave trading by European and American nations. It became a German and later a French colony. It gained its independence in 1960. It had the fastest economic growth rate of any African nation through the 1980s. Major products of Cameroon include oil, bauxite, iron, cocoa, coffee, and cotton.

Central African Republic is one of the few landlocked (it has no coastline) nations of Africa. It contains regions of rain forest and savanna. A wide range of vegetation grows there. Major crops include cotton, coffee, and rubber. Mineral resources, including coal, diamonds, iron ore, and uranium, are beginning to be developed. The nation gained its independence in 1960.

The Democratic Republic of the Congo was known as Zaire until 1997. It was a Belgian colony from the 1880s until its independence in 1960. Most of the region's population are farmers. A large dam on the Congo (Zaire) River provides hydroelectric power. The Congo has many mineral resources including copper, diamonds, gold, and iron. About half of the Congo is covered by forests. Wood exports are a major part of its economy.

Ghana was a British colony for 113 years before its independence in 1957. The official language of Ghana is still English. Ghana's main crops are cacao and coffee; its major industries are mining and light manufacturing. Gold and diamonds are both mined there. Ghana native Kofi Annan became the Secretary General of the United Nations in 1997.

The Ivory Coast is the world's largest producer of cacao, which is the source of chocolate and cocoa. It is also the world's third-largest producer of coffee. The former capital, Abidjan, is an important industrial center. The Ivory Coast was a French colony for many years before its independence in 1960. It still retains strong ties with France.

Liberia is the oldest Black republic in Africa. It was settled in 1822 by freed slaves from the United States. It became a republic in 1847. English is Liberia's official language. Liberia's major industry is its large rubber plantations. After many violent changes of government, Ruth Perry became Africa's first female head of state in 1996.

Nigeria is the most populous nation in Africa and the tenth most populous in the world. Nigeria became one of the world's largest exporters of oil after the discovery of huge reserves of oil and natural gas. Formerly a colony of Britain, Nigeria became independent in 1960.

Sierra Leone is a small nation bordering the Atlantic Ocean. Its climate is mainly tropical rain forest. It receives about 100 inches (2,540 mm) of precipitation during the rainy season. The British established Freetown in 1787 as a settlement for former slaves. Sierra Leone received independence from the British in 1961. Since independence, the nation has suffered many coups and civil wars. Major industries include mining and light manufacturing. Major crops include cacao, coffee, and rice.

DID YOU KNOW?

The Ivory Coast got its name because ivory from the tusks of elephants used to be traded along its coast.

Name: _____ Date: _____

Questions for Consideration

1. What was the former name of the Congo?

   _____

2. Where do most of the people of west and central Africa live?

   _____

3. What nation is the world's largest supplier of cacao?

   _____

4. What is Africa's most populous nation?

   _____

5. What native of Ghana became the Secretary General of the United Nations?

   _____

Map Project

On the map, label the
following:

Cameroon
Central African Republic
The Congo (Democratic
  Republic of the Congo)
Ghana
Ivory Coast
Liberia
Nigeria
Sierra Leone

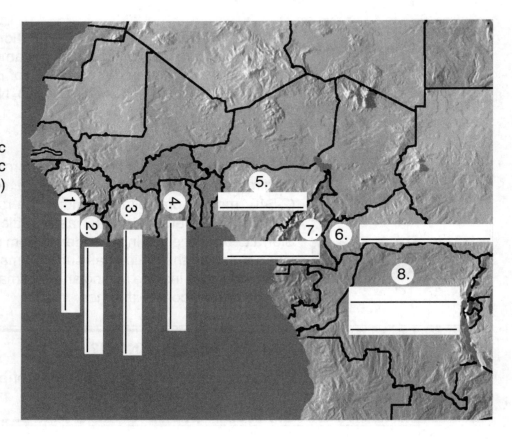

The Nations of East and Southern Africa

The nations of east and southern Africa include Angola, Botswana, Djibouti, Ethiopia, Kenya, Madagascar, Malawi, Somalia, South Africa, Sudan, Swaziland, Tanzania, Uganda, Zambia, and Zimbabwe.

Angola is one of Africa's larger countries. It has many natural resources. Major crops include bananas, coffee, cotton, sugar cane, and tobacco. Mineral deposits include diamonds, gold, iron ore, manganese, and oil. Angola received independence from Portugal in 1975. Angola, like many of the other African nations, has suffered political unrest since its independence.

Ethiopia is one of Africa's Christian nations. It also was one of the few African nations to avoid becoming a European colony. It produces coffee, figs, grapes, citrus fruits, and several grains. The highland area supports large herds of sheep and cattle. Ethiopia has suffered from droughts since the 1970s and suffered a severe famine in 1984. It has been the scene of many recent political uprisings.

Kenya received independence from Britain in 1963. Agriculture and tourism are Kenya's major industries. Kenya has many large national parks that serve as wildlife reserves. These national parks are popular tourist attractions. Kenya's major crops include coffee, corn, and tea. Its government remained stable until the early 1970s, when a series of civil wars broke out. Nairobi, Kenya's capital, was the site of the bombing of the United States Embassy in 1971.

Madagascar is a large island located in the Indian Ocean, off the southeast coast of Africa. Most of the island's population is of Asian rather than African descent. It was under French control from 1885 until 1960. Madagascar's major industry is agriculture. Its major products include cloves, coffee, cotton, and vanilla.

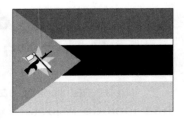

Mozambique became a colony of Portugal in the 1500s. After a ten-year struggle, the nation gained independence in 1975. In recent years, the nation has suffered from political unrest and severe droughts. Major crops include cashews, corn, cotton, sugar, and tea.

South Africa has a more varied and gentle climate than most of the rest of the continent. Its capital, Cape Town, is near Africa's southernmost point. South Africa is one of the world's richest nations in natural resources. It is the world's largest producer of diamonds. It also has large reserves of chromium, copper, iron ore, gold, manganese, nickel, platinum, and other minerals. South Africa was under British control from the early 1800s until 1910. In 1948, the government adopted a policy called apartheid to keep the racial groups separate. The human rights of non-Whites were severly limited. After years of protests from within and economic sanctions from other countries, apartheid was abandoned and multi-racial elections were held in 1994.

Sudan is Africa's largest nation. Sudan's capital, Khartoum, is located where the White Nile and Blue Nile Rivers merge. The northern and southern regions of the nation are quite different. Northern Sudan is hot and dry. Nubian clans inhabit the area. Northern Sudan has a mix of Arab and African cultures and has a strong Muslim influence. The southern region receives much rainfall. It is populated by numerous native ethnic groups. Sudan is primarily an agricultural economy. Cotton is the major export. The region suffered from major droughts in the 1970s and 1980s.

Tanzania was formed when the Republic of Tanganyika and the island Republic of Zanzibar joined in 1964. The nation is the world's largest producer of cloves. Tanzania was the site of a United States embassy bombing in 1998.

Uganda is the location of Africa's largest lake, Lake Victoria. Uganda was a British colony until its independence in 1962. Major crops include cotton, coffee, sugar, tea, and tobacco. Like many other African nations, Uganda suffered from many violent changes of government after independence.

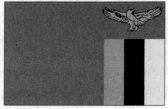

Zambia, which was formerly known as Northern Rhodesia, joined the Commonwealth of Nations, a group of nations with ties to Britain, after gaining its independence in 1964. The nation has large reserves of cobalt, copper, lead, manganese, and zinc. In spite of its mineral wealth, most of the population lives on small farms.

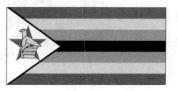

Zimbabwe was the British colony of Southern Rhodesia until it gained its independence in 1980. Zimbabwe is rich in minerals and farmlands; previously, however, civil wars have destroyed the nation's economy. It has recovered in recent years and may soon become one of Africa's leading nations.

Name: _____   Date: _____

Questions for Consideration

1. Which nation is one of Africa's major Christian nations?

   _____

2. Which African nation is noted for its large national parks and wildlife reserves?

   _____

3. What African nation is a large island?

   _____

4. What nation is the world's largest supplier of diamonds?

   _____

5. What nation is the world's largest supplier of cloves?

   _____

Map Project

On the map, label the following:

Angola   Ethiopia
Kenya   Madagascar
Mozambique   South Africa
Sudan   Tanzania
Zambia   Zimbabwe

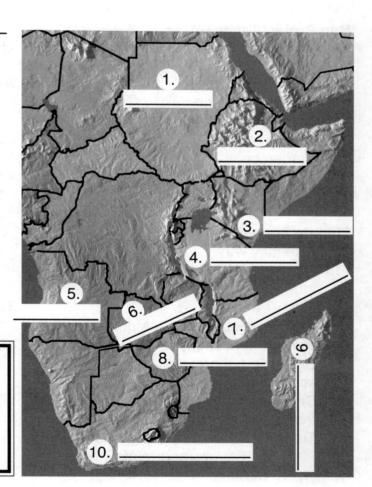

DID YOU KNOW?

The world's largest diamond mine was discovered near Pretoria, South Africa, in 1905.

Answer Keys

The Continents (page 3)
1. A large landmass completely or mostly surrounded by land
2. Just over 29 percent
3. Continental Drift Theory
4. Plate Tectonics
5. Volcanoes and earthquakes

Map Project (page 3)
Teacher check map.

The Continent of Africa (page 6)
1. Asia
2. The Nile
3. The Sahara
4. The equator
5. Queen Victoria of England

Map Project (page 6)
Teacher check map. Use map on page 5 as a guide.

Africa's Climate (page 8)
1. 94°F (34°C)
2. 51°F (11°C)
3. Cameroon
4. April to September
5. October to March

Climate Zones (page 8)
(Answers may vary.)
1. Desert: rainfall less than 10 inches (254 mm), temperatures over 90°F (32°C) to below freezing
2. Mediterranean: mild temperatures, wet winters, dry summers
3. Savanna: hot grassland, has a rainy season and a dry season
4. Steppe: dry, rainfall about 15 inches (381 mm) per year, most in one season
5. Tropical rain forest: average temperature 80°F (27°C), average rainfall 70 inches (1,778 mm)

Africa's Resources (page 10)
1. Titanium, uranium, and radium
2. Over one-half
3. Foreign nations
4. One-fifth
5. Japan, Russia, and the United States

Matching (page 10)
1. a
2. d
3. b
4. e
5. c

Africa's Industries (page 12)
1. It exports more than it imports.
2. Agriculture
3. The growing population
4. South Africa
5. Hydroelectric

Africa's Exports (page 12)
1. O   2. X   3. X   4. O
5. X   6. O   7. O   8. O
9. X   10. X

Africa's Animal Life (page 14)
1. The savanna
2. The illegal killing of animals
3. National parks
4. The tsetse fly
5. The ibis

The People of Africa (page 16)
1. 12 percent
2. Cairo, Egypt
4. Over 3,000
5. About 70 percent
6. Christianity, Islam, and Native Traditional

Answer Keys

Vocabulary (page 16)
(Answers will vary.)
1. Diverse: various, different
2. Indigenous: originally from a region
3. Kinship: a related group
4. Anthropologist: one who studies human beings, their works, and cultures
5. Literacy: ability to read (and write)

African Culture (page 18)
1. Islam
2. Traditional native
3. Kente
4. Rhythm
5. Wole Soyina

Matching (page 18)
1. d
2. c
3. e
4. a
5. b

The Nations of Northern Africa (page 21)
1. The Mediterranean Sea
2. Arabs and Berbers
3. The Nile River
4. Tripoli
5. Morocco

Map Project (page 21)
1. Atlantic Ocean
2. Morocco
3. Algeria
4. Tunisia
5. Libya
6. Egypt
7. Mediterranean Sea
8. Red Sea

The Nations of West and Central Africa (page 24)
1. Zaire
2. Along the Atlantic Ocean coast
3. The Ivory Coast
4. Nigeria
5. Kofi Annan

Map Project (page 24)
1. Sierra Leone
2. Liberia
3. Ivory Coast
4. Ghana
5. Nigeria
6. Central African Republic
7. Cameroon
8. the Congo (Democratic Republic of the Congo)

The Nations of East and Southern Africa (page 27)
1. Ethiopia
2. Kenya
3. Madagascar
4. South Africa
5. Tanzania

Map Project (page 27)
1. Sudan
2. Ethiopia
3. Kenya
4. Tanzania
5. Angola
6. Zambia
7. Mozambique
8. Zimbabwe
9. Madagascar
10. South Africa

Bibliography

Books for Young Adults:

Addison, John. *Traditional Africa.* Greenhaven, 1988.

Ayittey, G.B.N. *Africa Betrayed.* St. Martin's Press, 1992.

Boamah-Wiafe, Daniel. *Africa Today: Its Peoples and Contemporary Cultures.* Kendall-Hunt, 1988.

Buettner, Dan. *Africatrec: A Journey by Bicycle Through Africa.* Lerner Publishers, 1997.

Fetner, P.J. *The African Safari.* St. Martin's Press, 1987.

Harden, Blane. *Africa: Dispatches from a Fragile Continent.* Norton, 1990.

Haskins, James. *African Beginnings.* Lothrop, Lee, & Shepherd Books, 1998.

Haskins, James. *From Afar to Zulu: A Dictionary of African Cultures.* Lothrop, Lee, & Shepherd Books, 1995.

Ibazebo, Isimene. *Exploration into Africa.* New Discovery Books, 1994.

Lye, Keith. *Africa.* Glouschester Press, 1987.

Rowell, Trevor. *The Scramble for Africa.* B.T. Batsford, 1986.

Temko, Florence. *Traditional Crafts from Africa.* Lerner Publishers, 1996.